Pre-K

Jumbo Workbook

This workbook belongs to

Use pencils, crayons, and stickers to complete the activities in this book. When there is a sticker missing, you will see this pattern:

T0016576

Dear Parents,

Welcome to the *Jumbo Pre-K Workbook*!

Here are some tips to help ensure that your child gets the most from this book.

★ Look at the pages with your child, ensuring he or she knows what to do before starting.

★ Plan short, regular sessions, only doing one or two pages at a time.

★ Praise your child's efforts and improvements.

★ Encourage your child to assess his or her own efforts in a positive way. For example, say: "You've written some great A's there. Which one do you think you did best?"

★ Make the learning sessions positive experiences. Give prompts where they might help. If a section is too hard for your child, leave those pages until he or she is ready for them.

★ Relate the learning to things in your child's world. For example, if your child is working on a page about the color red, ask him or her to find some red things in your home.

★ There are stickers to use throughout the book. They help build your child's hand-eye coordination and observation skills. Encourage your child to place the stickers on each page before starting the other activities.

Together, the activities in the workbook help build a solid understanding of early learning concepts to ensure your child is ready for kindergarten and first grade.

We wish your child hours of enjoyment with this fun workbook!

Scholastic Early Learning

Contents

Heading home

Trace the lines from left to right.
Start at the big red dot.

Oscar

Mabel

Milo

Lily

A rainy day

Trace the lines from top to bottom.

Beach fun

Trace the sand castle.

Zigzag pattern

Trace the pattern on the sweater.

A stormy night

Trace the lightning bolts.

Beautiful rugs

Trace the patterns on the rugs.

Pretty flowers

Trace the petals.

Sea horses

Trace the lines on the sea horses.

A w v sea

Trace the waves.

Home, tweet home

Trace the path to the birdhouse.

Lovely lemonade

Trace the lemon slices.

Yo-yo fun

Trace the yo-yos.

Zigzag trail

Trace the path to the barn.

Loop the loop

Trace the lines to make the planes loop the loop.

Snail trails

Trace the trails to follow the snails.

Find my house

Trace the paths to find the correct homes.

Snowboard tricks

Trace the snowboarder's path.

Follow the scent

Trace the trail to find the child.

Rocket ride

Trace Rocky the Robot's journey to the moon.

Rabbit run

Trace the burrows to reach the rabbits.

Fly away

Help the plane fly from London to New York.

Start →

→ Finish

Lost in Space

Help the alien find his friends.

Start →

→ Finish

On track

Help the train reach the station.

Start →

PLATFORM N°1

→ Finish

Dino search

Help the dinosaur find her friend.

Start →

→ Finish

Time for bed

Help the puppy find his doghouse.

Start

Oscar

Finish

All aboard!

Help the pirate through the waves
to reach his ship.

Start →

→ Finish

Be a hero

Help the superhero reach his sidekick.

Start ➞

Finish ➞

Garden friends

Help the snail meet up with the ladybug.

Start

Finish

Find the joey

Help the kangaroo find her joey.

Start →

→ Finish

Home, sweet home

Help the girl find her way home.

Start →

Finish

An icy path

Help the penguin find his friends.

Start

Finish ←

Zoo games

Find your way through
the zebra's stripes.

Start

Finish

Tasty treat

Help the worm eat his way through the apple.

Start

Finish

Tree trail

Help the bird reach her nest.

Start

Finish

School run

Help the bus pick up all the children and get to school.

Start →

→ Finish

SCHOOL

Woodland walk

Help the deer through the forest without passing any wolves.

Start →

→ Finish

Robot race

Help the robot through the machine.

Start

Finish

Snack time

Help the children reach the ice-cream van.

Start →

→ Finish

Treasure hunt

Help the digger find the buried treasure
without passing any ants.

Start

Finish

Hungry squirrel

Help the squirrel down the tree,
picking up all the acorns on its way.

Start

Finish

Red and blue

Draw lines from the **red** things to the word **red**.
Draw lines from the **blue** things to the word **blue**.

Yellow and green

Put a **Y** by each yellow object.
Put a **G** by each green object.

Purple and orange

Draw lines from the **purple** things to the word **purple**.
Draw lines from the orange things to the word orange.

purple

orange

White and black

Put a **W** by each **white** object.
Put a **B** by each **black** object.

Where is it?

Sticker the dog **outside** the house.
Sticker the cat **inside** the house.

Color the car that
is **in front red**.
Color the car that
is **behind** blue.

High and low

Sticker the girl in the **top** bunk.
Sticker the boy in the **bottom** bunk.

Put an **H** by the monkey
that is up **high**.
Put an **L** by the monkey
that is down **low**.

Above and below

Sticker the teddy bear **on** the bed.
Sticker the shoes **under** the bed.

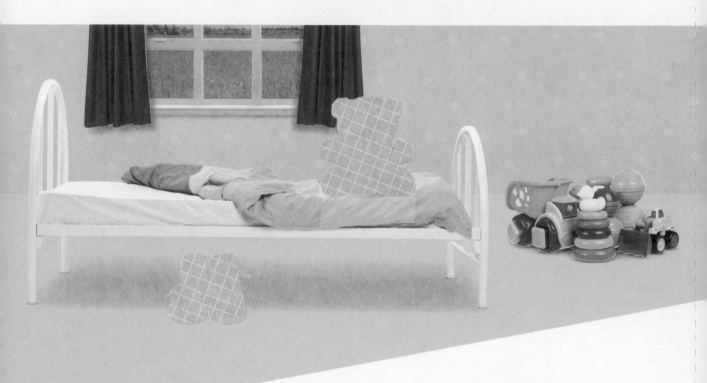

Draw a bird
above the boat.
Draw a fish
below the boat.

Signs to follow

Trace **stop** on the stop sign.
Trace **go** on the go sign.

STOP

GO

Trace **up** on the arrow pointing up.
Trace **down** on the arrow pointing down.

up

down

First and last

Put a check ✔ by the car
that came **first**.
Put a cross ✖ by the car
that came **last**.

Check ✔ the tree
that is **nearby**.
Put a cross ✖ by the tree
that is **far away**.

Size words

Circle the correct one in each box.

Circle the **big** dog.

Circle the **little** top.

Circle the **large** ball.

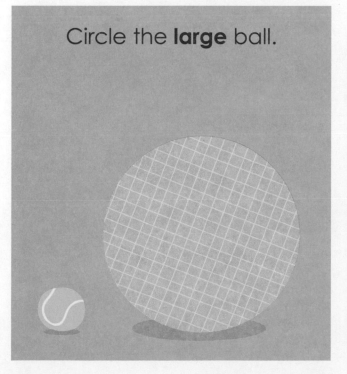

Circle the **small** insect.

More size words

Circle the correct one in each box.

Circle the **taller** boy.

Circle the **shorter** girl.

Circle the **longer** pencil.

Circle the **shorter** crayon.

How much?

Circle the correct one in each box.

Circle the glass that is **full**.

Circle the pitcher that is **empty**.

Circle the jar with **more** candy than the other.

Circle the plate with **less** cake than the other.

Weather words

Trace the weather words.

 It is sunny.

It is rainy.

 It is cold.

 It is windy.

Weather match

Draw lines to match each child to the weather.

sunny

rainy

cold

windy

The seasons

Finish coloring the summer picture.

Finish coloring the fall picture.

The seasons

Finish coloring the winter picture.

Finish coloring the spring picture.

Summer clothes

Circle the clothes Ben wears in **summer**.

coat

sandals

T-shirt

sunglasses

gloves

woolly hat

scarf

swimming trunks

Winter clothes

Circle the clothes Ella wears in **winter**.

sweater

hat

boots

scarf

coat

sunglasses

T-shirt

woolly hat

Happy or sad?

Circle the face that goes with the picture.

Match the emotions

Draw lines to match the faces to the emojis.

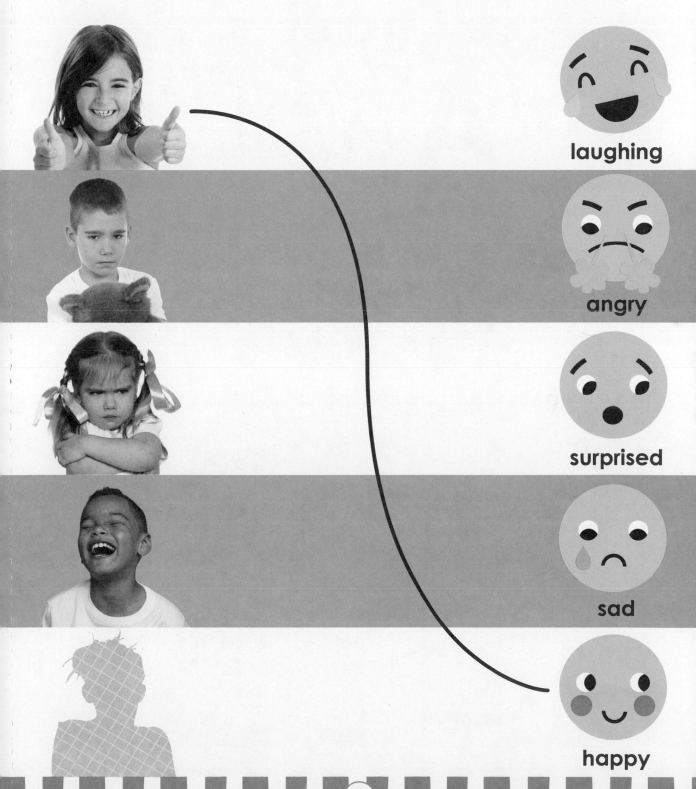

laughing

angry

surprised

sad

happy

Uppercase letters

Circle the letters. One has been circled for you.

(A) G

X T P

K H D

M L B

Lowercase letters

Circle the letters.

a  b  d

s  w

 h i

m k o

Find the words

Words are made up of letters joined together. Circle the words.

dog

go

is

me

big

fun

see

look

Find the words

Circle the words.

egg ★ play

was

hen

in

run no

can

yes

Sort letters and words

Circle the words with a **red** pencil.
Circle the letters with a **blue** pencil.

bee   b   x

fish   j

u   bus

h   nose   f   cat

ball   car

k   w   moon

Find the letters

Draw a line from each letter in the word
to the same letter around it.

p

i

a

b ——— **bird**

d

u

w

r

z

b

t

boat

h

a

o

Find uppercase letters

Find and circle the letter **S**.

R Z S B O Q

Spider

Find and circle the letter **L**.

K T C I L J

Lion

Find and circle the letter **O**.

D P O C G

Octopus

Find and circle the letter **F**.

Y R F T P E

Fish

Find lowercase letters

Find and circle the letter **h**.

t h b k d f

house

Find and circle the letter **m**.

n W x h m h

mouse

Find and circle the letter **v**.

W u v Z x y

vet

Find and circle the letter **d**.

h b d q k p

dog

Match the direction

Circle the **c**'s that face the correct way.

cow

Circle the **b**'s that face the correct way.

b d **b** d b

ball

Circle the **p**'s that face the correct way.

q p p q p

panda

Circle the **s**'s that face the correct way.

s ƨ ƨ s ƨ

socks

Match the direction

Circle the **g**'s that face the correct way.

g e g g e

goat

Circle the **f**'s that face the correct way.

f f f f f

fox

Circle the **j**'s that face the correct way.

i j i j j j i

jacket

Circle the **h**'s that face the correct way.

h h d d h

hippo

Letter order

Circle the word **saw**. The letters must be in the correct order.

saw   was

saw

was

I **saw** a bird.

Circle the word **on**.

on   on

no

on

I am **on** a leaf.

Letter order

Circle the word **cat**.

I am a **cat**.

cat
tac
act
cat

Circle the word **big**.

I am a **big** dog.

gib
big
big
gib

First words

Trace the words.

sun   dog   ball

car   cap   mug

First words

Trace the words.

star drum duck

leaf dress fish

Match the words

Draw lines to match the words that are the same.

 owl

 fox

 tree

 bird

 **deer**

 owl

 bird

 bee

 bee

 tree

 fox

 **deer**

Match the words

Draw lines to match the words that are the same.

 shell | whale

 shark | fish

 crab | shark

 fish | boat

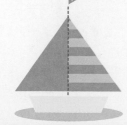 whale | crab

boat | shell

Write sentences

Sentences are made up of words.
Trace the sentences.

I am a cat.

I am a dog.

I am a bat.

I am a frog.

Write sentences

Trace the sentences.

This is a car.

This is a king.

This is a star.

This is a ring.

Color the **A**. Then trace the dotted letters.

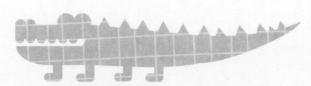

ant   apple   alligator

Color the **B**. Then trace the dotted letters.

bike   bear   bus

Color the **C**. Then trace the dotted letters.

C c C c

cap   car   cactus

Color the **D**. Then trace the dotted letters.

D d D d

dragon   drum   dog

Color the **E**. Then trace the dotted letters.

E E e E e

egg elephant engine

Color the **F**. Then trace the dotted letters.

F F f F f

fox flower fish

Color the **G**. Then trace the dotted letters.

GgGg

giraffe gift guitar

Color the **H**. Then trace the dotted letters.

HhHh

hat heart hippo

I

Color the **I**. Then trace the dotted letters.

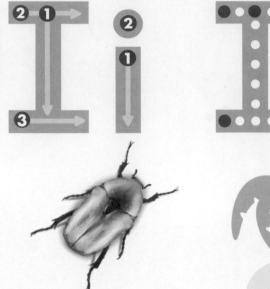

igloo   insect   island

J

Color the **J**. Then trace the dotted letters.

jacket   jewels   jet

K

Color the **K**. Then trace the dotted letters.

K k k K k

kitten   kite   key

L

Color the **L**. Then trace the dotted letters.

L l l L l

lizard   leaf   lion

Color the **M**. Then trace the dotted letters.

M Mm Mm

mouse milk monster

Color the **N**. Then trace the dotted letters.

N Nn Nn

net noodles nine

Color the **O**. Then trace the dotted letters.

otter octopus orange

Color the **P**. Then trace the dotted letters.

pirate pear pony

Color the **Q**. Then trace the dotted letters.

quail   quilt   queen

Color the **R**. Then trace the dotted letters.

rocket   robot   rabbit

Color the **S**. Then trace the dotted letters.

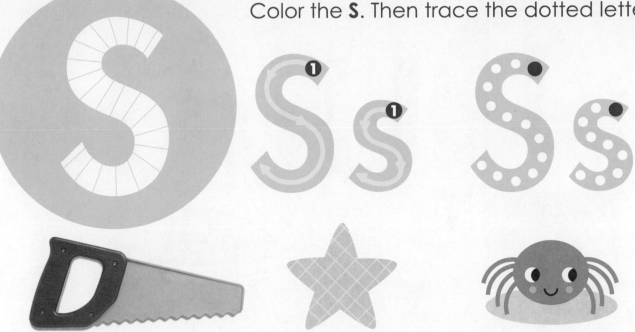

saw   star   spider

Color the **T**. Then trace the dotted letters.

tiger   truck   tree

Color the **U**. Then trace the dotted letters.

UuUu

unicorn   umbrella

Color the **V**. Then trace the dotted letters.

VvVv

volcano   vase   van

Color the **W**. Then trace the dotted letters.

WwWw

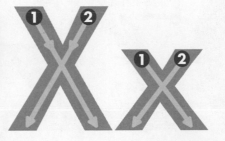

whale watch wolf

Color the **X**. Then trace the dotted letters.

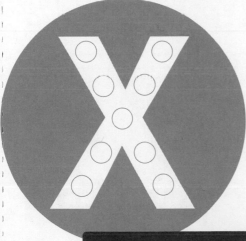

XxXx

 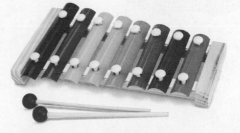

X-ray xylophone

Color the **Y**. Then trace the dotted letters.

yawn   yo-yo   yogurt

Color the **Z**. Then trace the dotted letters.

zero   zoo   zebra

Lowercase dot-to-dot

Join the letters in alphabetical order. Start at **a**.

Uppercase maze

Help Ted reach the picnic by following the letters in alphabetical order. Say the letters aloud as you go.

Start

A B C D E

F

J I H G H

K

L M N O P

Finish

Z Q

Y T U R S

X W V U T

Lowercase maze

Help the race car reach the finish by following the letters in alphabetical order. Say the letters aloud as you go.

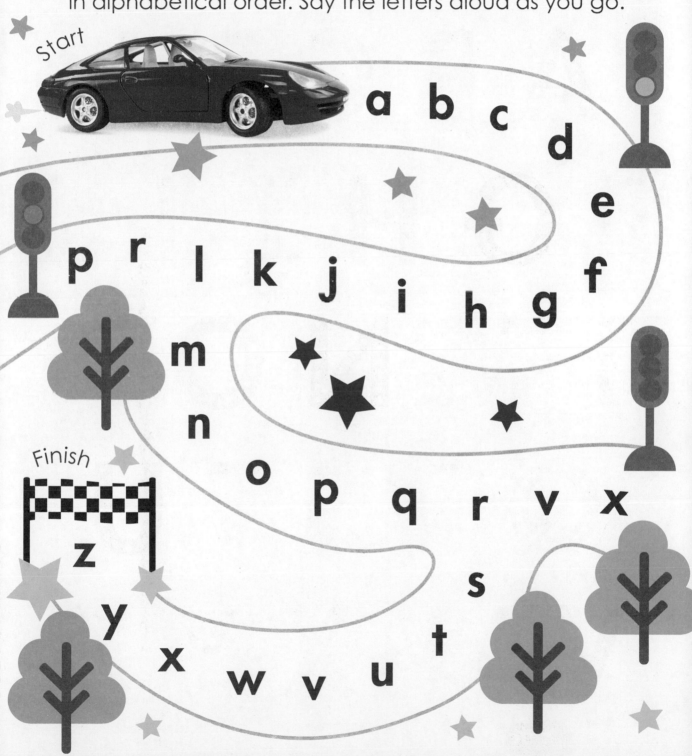

The uppercase letters

Trace the uppercase letters.

The lowercase letters

Trace the lowercase letters.

a b c d e
f g h i j k
l m n o p
q r s t u
v w x y z

Color the **s**. Then say the **s** words aloud.

soap   sock

snail   slide

Say the sentence aloud, and then trace the **s**'s.

seesaw

Sam

Spot

Sam sits on the seesaw.

Color the **t**. Then say the **t** words aloud.

tiger

tent

train

truck

Say the sentence aloud, and then trace the **t**'s.

turtle

tomato

Tia's turtle eats a tomato.

Color the **p**. Then say the **p** words aloud.

pig

push

puppet pumpkin

Say the sentence aloud, and then trace the **p**'s.

piano

Pip

Pip plays the piano.

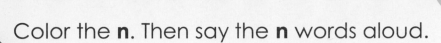
Color the **n**. Then say the **n** words aloud.

nose  nuts

 necklace  nap

Say the sentence aloud, and then trace the **n**'s.

Nina night nurse

Nina is a nice nurse.

Color the **m**. Then say the **m** words aloud.

m

mask **m**ilk

 **m**ouse **m**ug

Say the sentence aloud, and then trace the **m**'s.

mermaid

Mia

Mia met a mermaid.

Color the **d**. Then say the **d** words aloud.

deer

desk

duck

dress

Say the sentence aloud, and then trace the **d**'s.

dog

Dan

deck

Dan dozes on the deck.

Color the **g**. Then say the **g** words aloud.

goose goat

gold girl

Say the sentence aloud, and then trace the **g**'s.

Grace

gift

Grace gets a good gift.

Color the **c**. Then say the **c** words aloud.

corn

coin

car

cow

Say the sentence aloud, and then trace the **c**'s.

cut

cat

cake

The **c**at **c**ut the **c**ake.

Color the **k**. Then say the **k** words aloud.

kitten

king

kick

kilt

Say the sentence aloud, and then trace the **k**'s.

kite

Karl

koala

Karl the koala flies a kite.

Color the **r**. Then say the **r** words aloud.

r robot ring

r rose rocket

Say the sentence aloud, and then trace the **r**'s.

rain

race

rabbit

The rabbits run a race.

Color the **h**. Then say the **h** words aloud.

hare

hat

house

hammer

Say the sentence aloud, and then trace the letters.

horse

Hallie

hay

Hallie's horse likes hay.

Color the **b**. Then say the **b** words aloud.

b bird

b boy

b boat

b ball

Say the sentence aloud, and then trace the letters.

bats

ball

Ben

Ben bats the blue ball.

Color the **f**. Then say the **f** words aloud.

fox   fork

fan   feather

Say the sentence aloud, and then trace the **f**'s.

Fay

fish

Fay sees five fab fish.

Color the **l**. Then say the **l** words aloud.

lion lamp

lemon leaf

Say the sentence aloud, and then trace the l's.

Liam

lunch

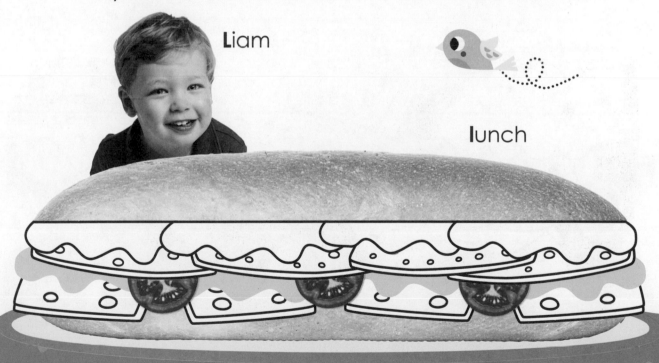

Look at Liam's long lunch.

Color the **j**. Then say the **j** words aloud.

j

jar

jet

juice

jeans

Say the sentence aloud, and then trace the **j**'s.

jeep

Julie

Jack

Jack likes Julie's jeep.

Color the **v**. Then say the **v** words aloud.

vase   violin

violet   van

Say the sentence aloud, and then trace the **v**'s.

Victor   vet

Victor visits the vet.

Color the **w**. Then say the **w** words aloud.

wood

web

worm

wink

Say the sentence aloud, and then trace the **w**'s.

walrus

wave

Will

Will waves at a walrus.

Color the **y**. Then say the **y** words aloud.

 yogurt

 yell

 yak

 yawn

Say the sentence aloud, and then trace the **y**'s.

Yuri

yellow

yo-yo

Yasmine

Yuri has a yellow yo-yo.

Color the **q**. Then say the **q** words aloud.

quack quail

quilt quiet

Say the sentence aloud, and then trace the letters.

quiz

queen

The queen took a quiz.

Color the **x**. Then say the **x** words aloud.

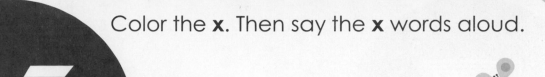

X

X-ray

box

xylophone

ox

Say the sentence aloud, and then trace the letters.

fox

Max

Max saw six foxes.

Color the **z**. Then say the **z** words aloud.

Z

buzz!

buzz **zigzag**

zoo **0 zero**

Say the sentence aloud, and then trace the **z**'s.

Zac

zebra

Zac the zebra zooms by.

Word match

Circle the word that matches the picture.

pen （hen）

rock sock

nail mail

wall ball

frog log

Trace **-all** in these words.

-all

ball

fall

call

wall

Add **-all** to the sentence.

They all
play ball.

Trace **-an** in these words.

Circle the word that matches the picture.

van jam | hen **man**

Trace **-at** in these words.

-at

cat

hat

rat

bat

Add **-at** to the sentence.

I can pat the cat.

Trace **-ay** in these words.

-ay ① ① ②

play

tray

jay

hay

Circle the word that matches the picture.

clap clay | **spray boy**

Trace **-eep** in these words.

-eep

sweep

cheep

sleep

peep

Add **-eep** to the sentence.

Beep! goes the jeep.

Trace **-en** in these words.

Draw lines from the **-en** words to the **-en**.

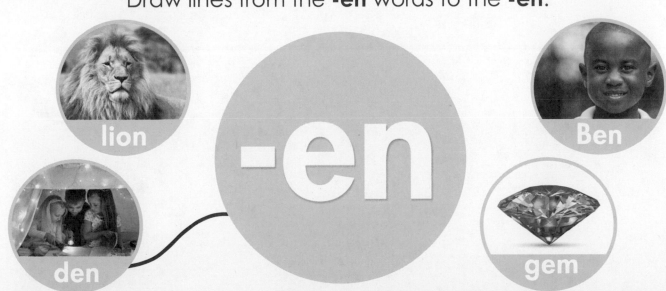

Trace **-et** in these words.

net

wet

jet

vet

Add **-et** to the sentence.

My pet met the vet.

Trace **-ick** in these words.

-ick chick sick brick lick

Circle the word that matches the picture.

kick kite

stop stick

Trace **-ill** in these words.

drill

spill

hill

ill

Add **-ill** to the sentence.

Jill will climb a hill.

130

Trace -in in these words.

-in   pin   win   twins   grin

Circle the word that matches the picture.

chin   sun | **skip   spin**

Trace **-ing** in these words.

-ing

wing

ring

string

swing

Add **-ing** to the sentence.

I sing in my ring.

Trace -ip in these words.

-ip

skip

flip

sip

lips

Circle the word that matches the picture.

pig snip

ship fish

Trace **-it** in these words.

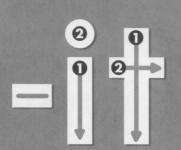

sit

fit

knit

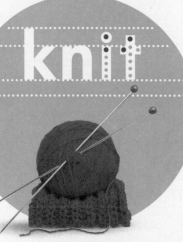

hit

Add **-it** to the sentence.

Kit can hit it.

Trace **-og** in these words.

Draw lines from the **-og** words to the **-og**.

bag

doll

-og

cog

dog

Trace **-ook** in these words.

rook

hook

book

look

Add **-ook** to the sentence.

The cook has a book.

Trace -op in these words.

-op ① ①

crop

pop

hop

stop

Circle the word that matches the picture.

top tap | map mop

Trace **-ot** in these words.

-ot

Spot

hot

pot

knot

Add **-ot** to the sentence.

Dot got too hot.

Trace **-ow** in these words.

Draw lines from the **-ow** words to the **-ow**.

Trace **-ug** in these words.

-ug

slug

bug

mug

hug

Add **-ug** to the sentence.

A pug tugs the rug.

Trace **-un** in these words.

-un

run

fun

sun

bun

Circle the word that matches the picture.

sun son

rub run

Trace the dotted letters.

Aa A A A A a a a

Read the **a** words and trace the picture.

ants

apple

anchor

Trace the dotted letters.

Bb B B B b b b

Read the **b** words and trace the picture.

bear

bird

ball

C c ① ①

Trace the dotted letters.

C C C C C C c c c

Read the **c** words and trace the picture.

cup

car

cat

D d ①②

Trace the dotted letters.

D D D D D d d d

Read the **d** words and trace the picture.

ducks

daisy

dog

Ee

Trace the dotted letters.

E E E E e e e

Read the **e** words and trace the picture.

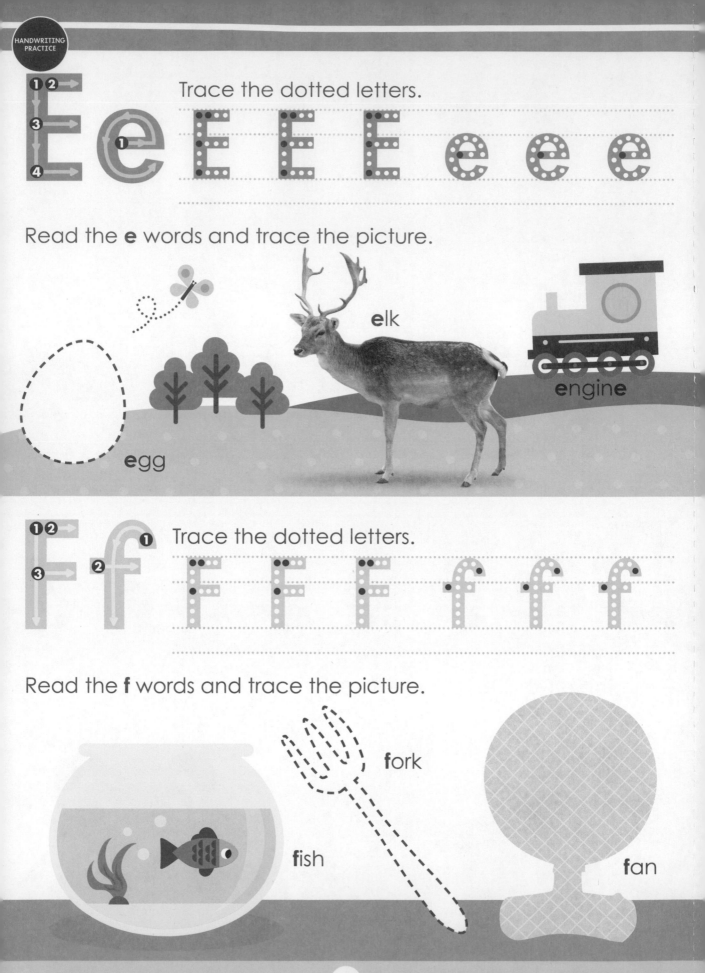

egg

elk

engin**e**

Ff

Trace the dotted letters.

F F F f f f

Read the **f** words and trace the picture.

fish

fork

fan

G g

Trace the dotted letters.

G G G g g g

Read the **g** words and trace the picture.

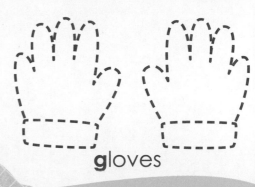

goose

goat

gloves

H h

Trace the dotted letters.

H H H h h h

Read the **h** words and trace the picture.

hippo

hat

house

Trace the dotted letters.

I I I I i i i

Read the **i** words and trace the picture.

igloo

insect

ice skates

Trace the dotted letters.

J J J J J J

Read the **j** words and trace the picture.

jeans

jaguar

jet

Kk

Trace the dotted letters.

K K K K k k k

Read the **k** words and trace the picture.

key

kitten

kangaroo

Trace the dotted letters.

L L L l l l

Read the **l** words and trace the picture.

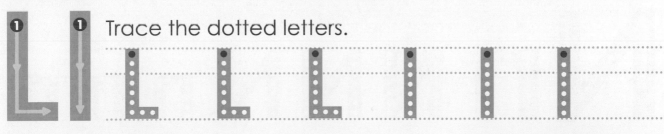

lemon

leaf

lion

Mm

Trace the dotted letters.

MMMMmmm

Read the **m** words and trace the picture.

moth

moon

mouse

Nn

Trace the dotted letters.

NNNNnnn

Read the **n** words and trace the picture.

necklace

nest

nut

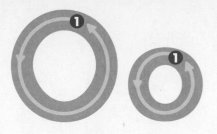

Trace the dotted letters.

Read the **o** words and trace the picture.

owl

orange

octopus

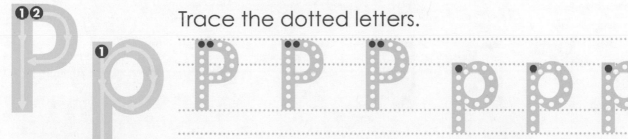

Trace the dotted letters.

Read the **p** words and trace the picture.

pumpkin

puppy

plane

Qq

Trace the dotted letters.

Q Q Q Q q q q

Read the q words and trace the picture.

queen

quiet

quilt

Rr

Trace the dotted letters.

R R R R r r r

Read the r words and trace the picture.

rocket

rose

ring

Trace the dotted letters.

Read the **s** words and trace the picture.

snake

scissors

star

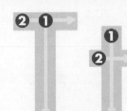

Trace the dotted letters.

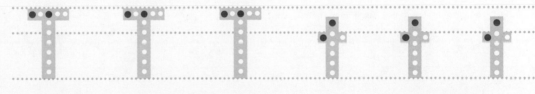

Read the **t** words and trace the picture.

tent

tiger

turtle

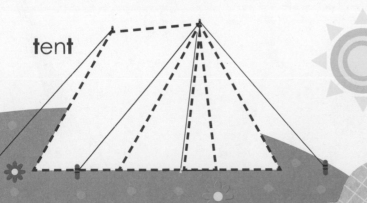

1 U u

Trace the dotted letters.

U u U U U U u u u

Read the **u** words and trace the arrow.

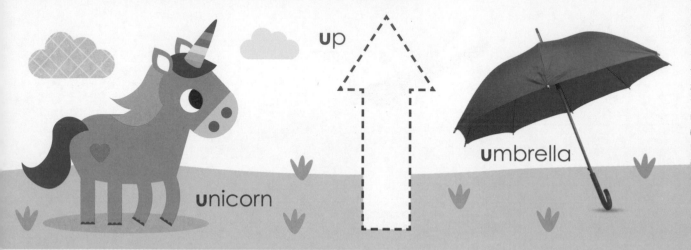

unicorn

up

umbrella

1 V v

Trace the dotted letters.

V v V V V V v v v

Read the **v** words and trace the picture.

vet

Viking

violin

Ww

Trace the dotted letters.

Ww WWwww

Read the **w** words and trace the picture.

worm

wheel

watch

Xx

Trace the dotted letters.

Xx XXXxxx

Read the **x** words and trace the picture.

xylophone

X-ray

fo**x**

Trace the dotted letters.

Read the **y** words and trace the picture.

yacht

yo-**y**o

yawn

Trace the dotted letters.

Read the **z** words and trace the picture.

zoo

zebra

zero

Say these short **a** words and trace the **a**'s.

bat

nap

rat

cap

can

man

Say these short **e** words and trace the **e**'s.

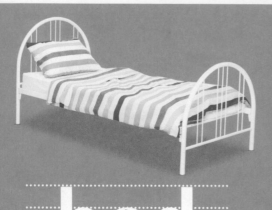

bed

hen

shell

bell

pen

wet

Say these short **i** words and trace the **i**'s.

dig

pig

twins

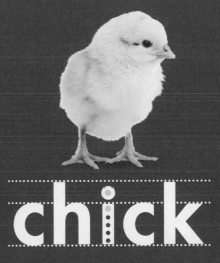

chick

lid

kick

Say these short **o** words and trace the **o**'s.

box

jog

frog

clock

sock

pot

Say these short **u** words and trace the **u**'s.

duck

mug

drum

sun

slug

truck

1

one

Color the **1**.
Then sticker and count **1 sun**.

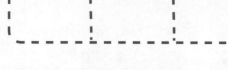

Trace the **1**'s.

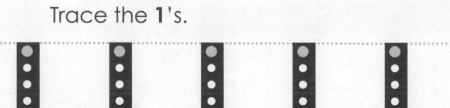

Trace the dotted line to find **1 bee**.

2
two

Color the **2**.
Then sticker and count **2 strawberries**.

Color the dinosaur to make **2 dinosaurs**.

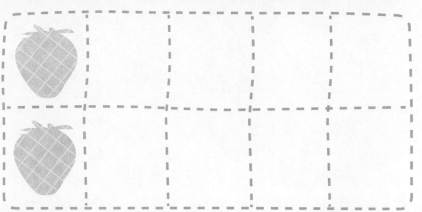

Trace the **2**'s.

three

Color the **3**.
Then sticker and count **3 cookies**.

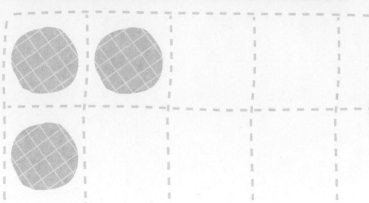

Trace the **3**'s.

① 3 3 3 3 3 3

Circle the plate with **3 cupcakes**.

four

Color the **4**.
Then sticker and count **4 flowers**.

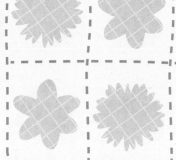

Trace and color **4 spots** on the ladybug.

Trace the **4**'s.

123

5
five

Color the **5**.
Then sticker, color, and count **5 faces**.

Trace the **5**'s.

5 5 5 5 5 5

Color **5 bananas** for the chimp.

six

Color the **6**.
Then sticker, color, and count **6 crowns**.

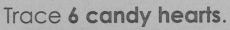

Trace **6 candy hearts**.

Trace the **6**'s.

7

seven

Color the **7**.
Then sticker, color, and count **7 balls**.

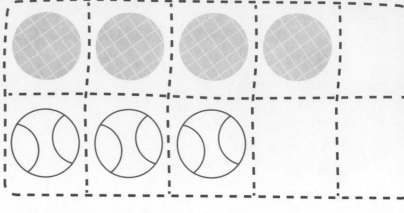

Trace the **7**'s.

Check the box by the pond with **7 ducks**.

eight

Color the **8**.
Then sticker, color, and count **8 apples**.

Trace the numbers to count the octopus's legs.

Trace the **8**'s.

9
nine

Color the **9**.
Then sticker, color, and count **9 butterflies**.

Trace the **9**'s.

9 9 9 9 9 9

Trace and color the sock to make **9 socks**.

10
ten

Color the **10**.
Then sticker, color, and count **10 stars**.

Trace the numbers to count the fingers.

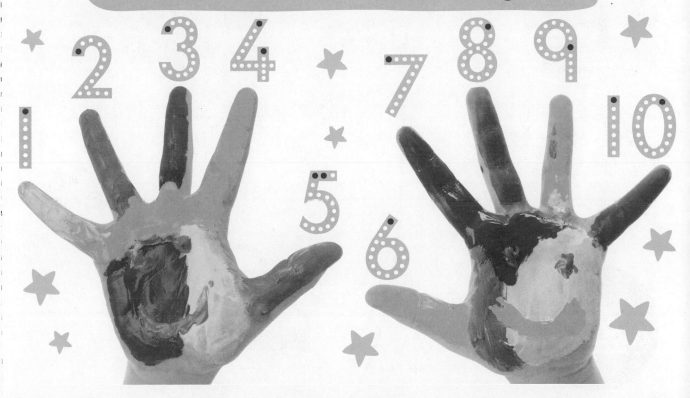

Trace the **10**'s.

Count and match

Trace the numbers, and draw lines to match the **numbers** to the **groups**.

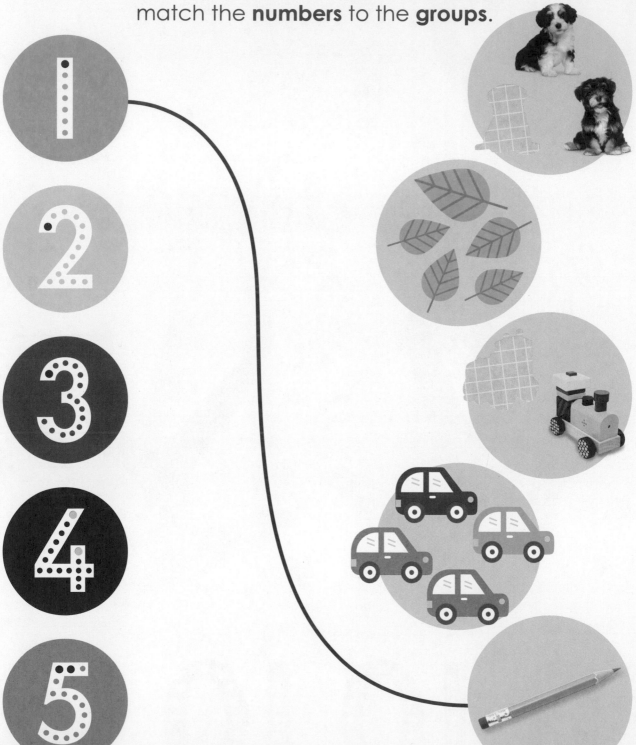

One more

Here are **3 butterflies**. Sticker **1** more to make **4 butterflies**.

Here are **5 Popsicles**. Sticker **1** more to make **6 Popsicles**.

Here are **7 balloons**. Sticker **1** more to make **8 balloons**.

One less

Here are **4 diggers**. Cross out **1** to make **3 diggers**.

Here are **6 crabs**. Cross out **1** to make **5 crabs**.

Here are **10 hats**. Cross out **1** to make **9 hats**.

Counting to 15

Count **11 flowers**. Color the last **1**.

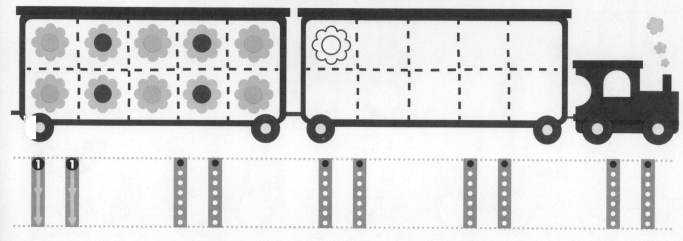

Count **12 trees**. Color the last **2**.

Count **13 birds**. Sticker the last **3**.

Count **14 stars**. Color the last **4**.

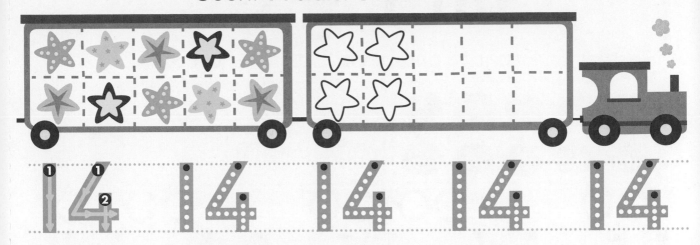

Count **15 balls**. Sticker the last **5**.

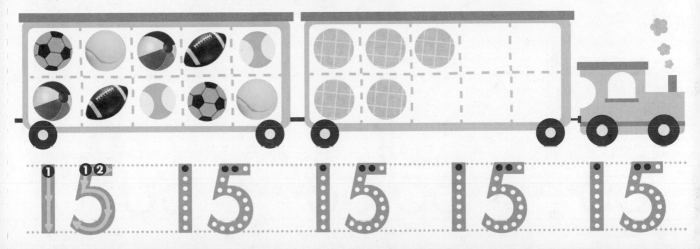

Trace the numbers from **11** to **15**.

Counting to 20

Count **16 pumpkins**. Color the last **6**.

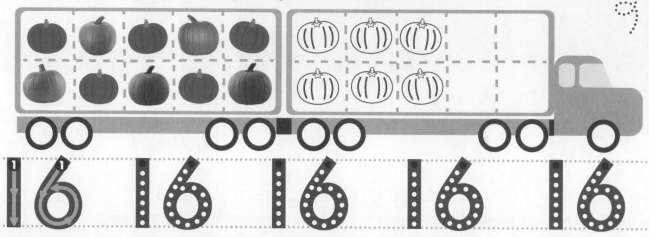

Count **17 lemons**. Color the last **7**.

Count **18 frozen treats**. Sticker the last **8**.

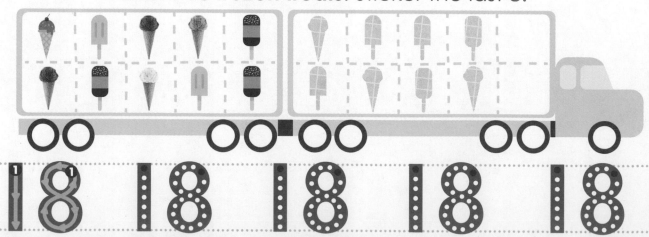

Count **19 cheese wedges**. Color the last **9**.

Count **20 cupcakes**. Sticker the last **10**.

Trace the numbers from **16** to **20**.

Dot-to-dot fun

Join the dots and finish coloring the picture.
Start at the colored dot.

Numbers to 20

Read and trace the numbers.

1 2 3 4 5

6 7 8 9 10

11 12 13 14 15

16 17 18 19 20

How many pieces of candy can you count?

Squares

Trace the **squares**.

Trace the **squares**.

Check the picture with a **square** frame.

Finish the **square** pattern.

Rectangles

Trace the **rectangles**.

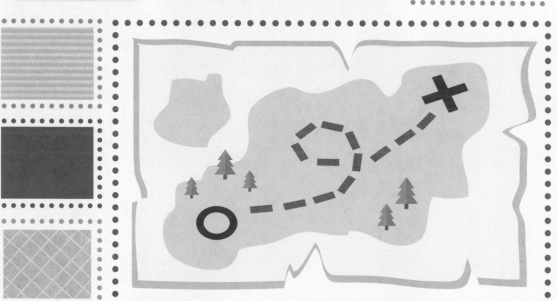

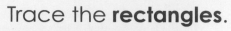

Trace the **rectangles**.

Check the **rectangular** cookie.

Finish the **rectangle** pattern.

Triangles

Trace the **triangles**.

Trace the **triangles**.

Check the **triangular** shape.

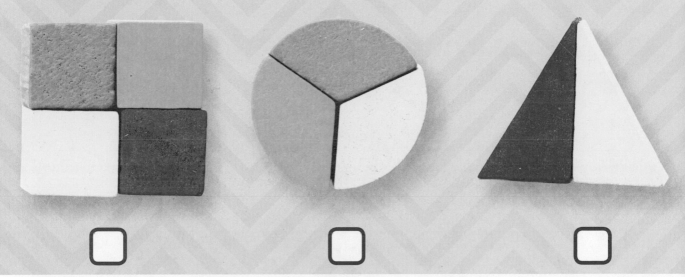

☐   ☐   ☐

Finish the **triangle** pattern.

Circles

Trace the **circles**.

Trace the **circles**.

Check the **circular** pieces of sports equipment.

Finish the **circle** pattern.

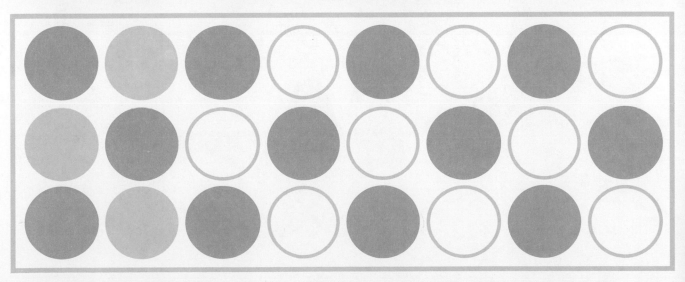

Stars

Trace the **stars**.

Trace the **stars**.

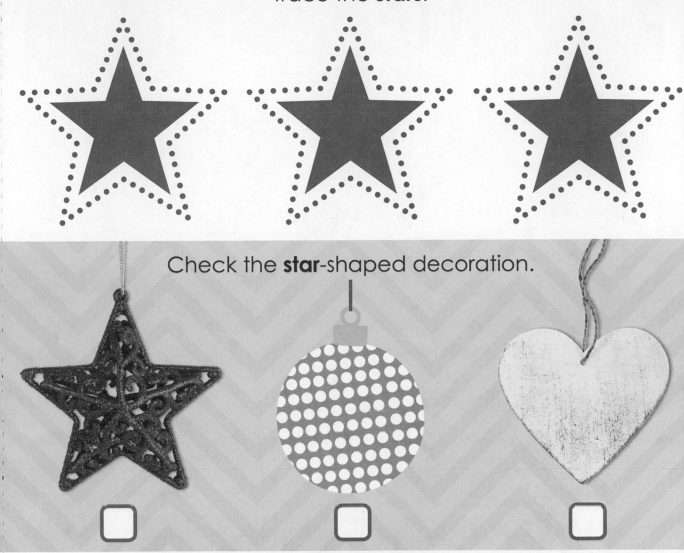

Check the **star**-shaped decoration.

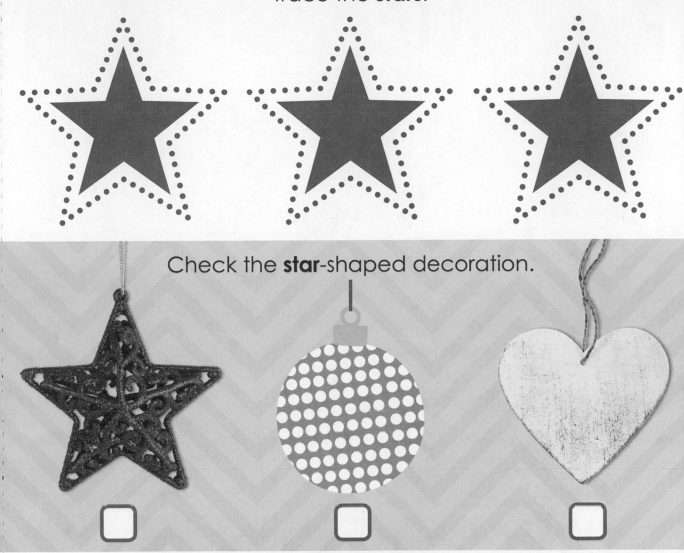

Finish the **star** pattern.

Hearts

Trace the **hearts**.

Trace the **hearts**.

Check the **heart**-shaped button.

Finish the **heart** pattern.

Matching shapes

Draw lines to join the shapes that are the same.

Matching objects

Draw lines to join the shapes and objects.

Shape patterns

Circle the shape that comes next in each row.

Picture patterns

Circle the picture that comes next in each row.

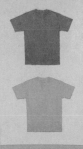

Shape patterns

Circle the shape that comes next in each row.

Picture patterns

Circle the picture that comes next in each row.

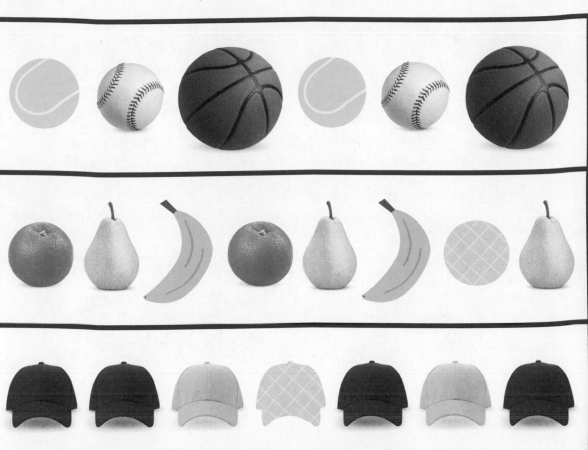

Match the animals

Draw lines to match the animals.

Draw lines to match the birds.

Match the toys

Draw lines to match the toys.

Draw lines to match the instruments.

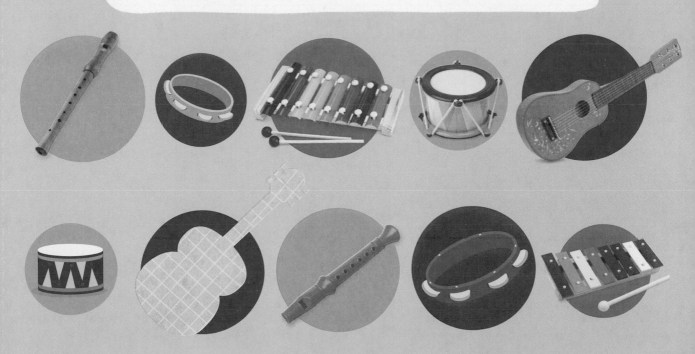

Match the caps

Sticker the matching cap beside each T-shirt.

Match the shapes

Draw lines to match the shapes.

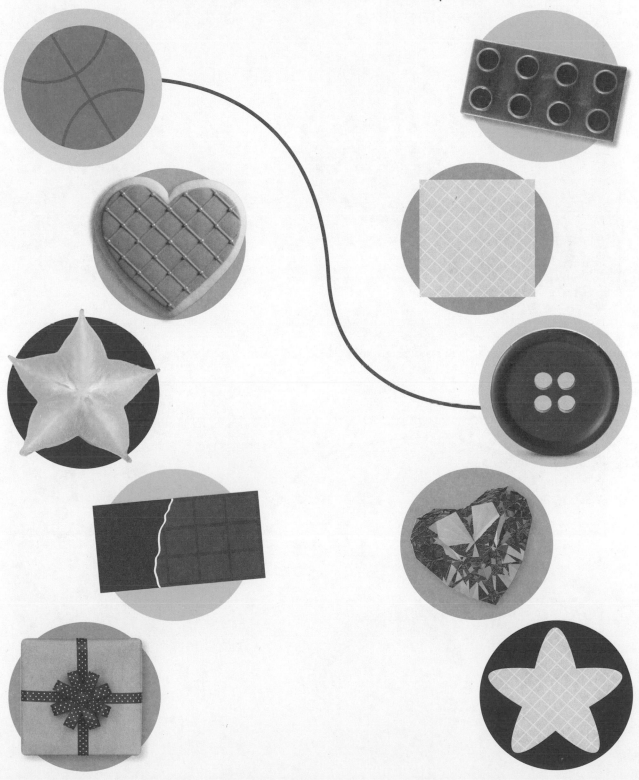

Sort the sizes

Draw lines from the small things to the word *small*.
Draw lines from the big things to the word *big*.

small

BIG

Match the clothes

Draw lines to match the pairs.

Find the pairs

Draw lines to match the things that are the same.

Find the pairs

Draw lines to match the things that are the same.

Mothers and babies

Draw lines to join the mothers and babies.

Find the lost items

Draw lines to join the people to their lost items.

Sort the vehicles

Draw lines to join the people with their vehicles.

Where does it go?

Draw lines from the toys to the toy box.
Draw lines from the books to the bookshelf.

Draw lines from the clean clothes to the drawers.
Draw lines from the dirty clothes to the laundry basket.

What's alive?

Circle the things that live and grow.

Sorting plants and animals

Draw lines from the animals to the animal group.
Draw lines from the plants to the plant group.

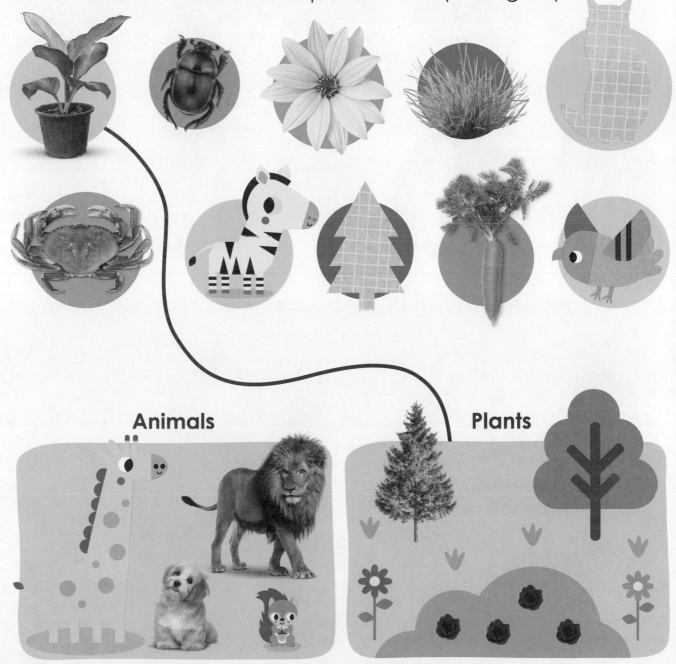

Animals

Plants

What doesn't belong?

Circle the one that's different in each row.

What doesn't belong?

Circle the one that's different in each row.

Summer and winter

Draw lines from the summer things to the sun.
Draw lines from the winter things to the snowflake.

What doesn't belong here?

Cross out the things that don't belong at the beach.

Find the differences

Can you find six differences between these pictures?

Match the opposites

Draw lines to match each thing to its opposite.

happy

empty

day

winter

up

sad

full

night

summer

down

Our bodies

Draw lines to show where each body part is on the boy.

mouth

hand

nose

ear

arm

head

stomach

foot

The senses

Draw lines to match the senses with the pictures.

smell

taste

touch

hear

see

Growing up

What comes first? Sticker the numbers **1** to **4** in order.

old person

child

baby

adult

Is it an animal?

Animals move, breathe, and eat. Circle the animals.

Is it an insect?

Insects have 6 legs. Circle the insects.

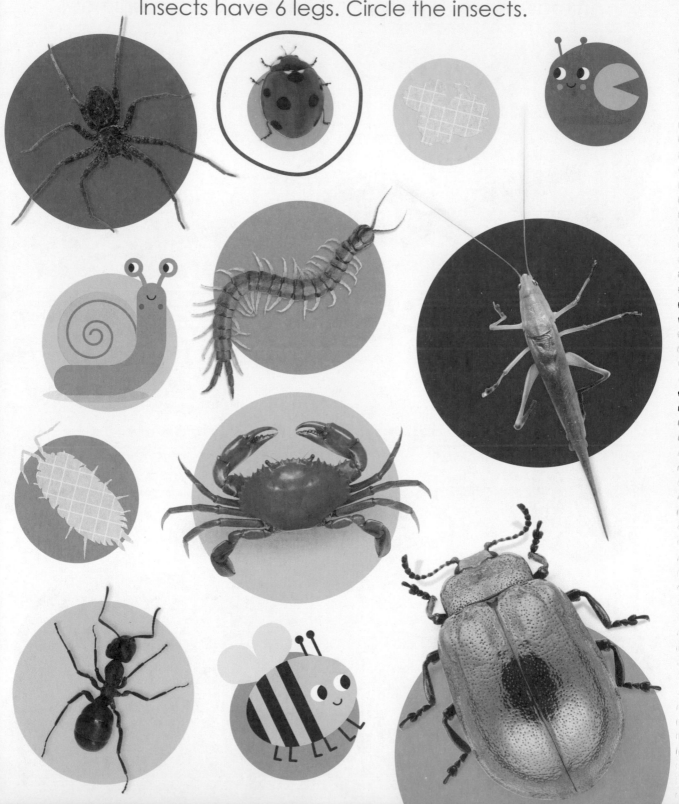

Where do we live?

Draw lines to match the places with the animals that live there.

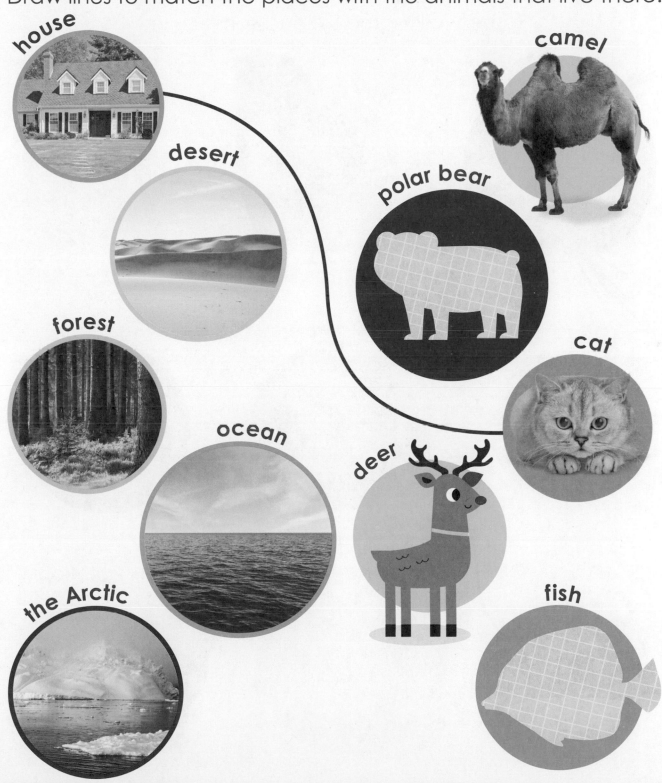

house

camel

desert

polar bear

forest

cat

ocean

deer

the Arctic

fish

How do we move?

Draw lines to join the animals that move in the same way.
Some walk, some fly, and some swim.

bird

dog

fish

jellyfish

butterfly

lizard

bat

dolphin

lion

Who's in my family?

Draw lines to join the animals from the same family.

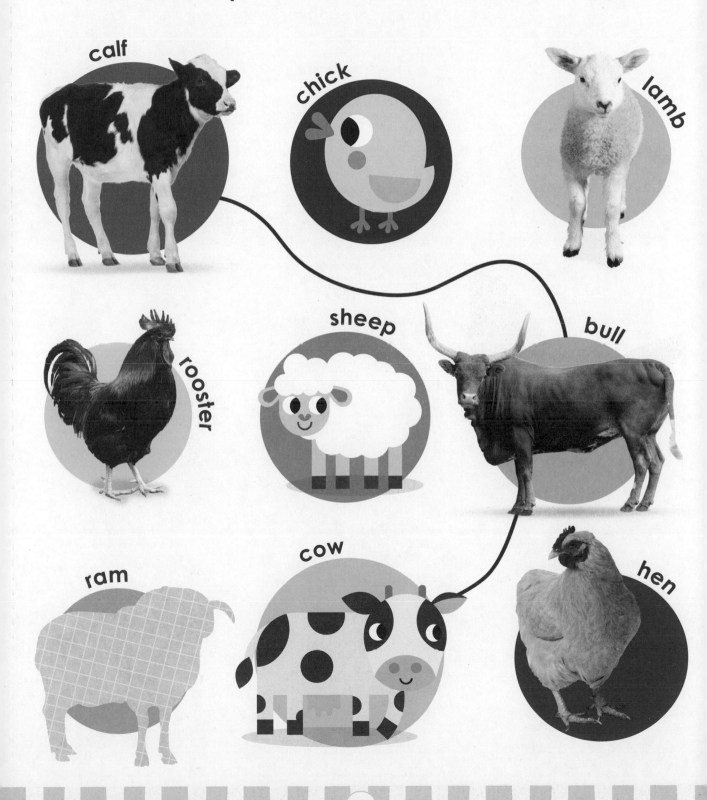

calf

chick

lamb

rooster

sheep

bull

ram

cow

hen

Butterfly life cycle

What comes first? Sticker the numbers **1** to **4**
on the butterfly life cycle.

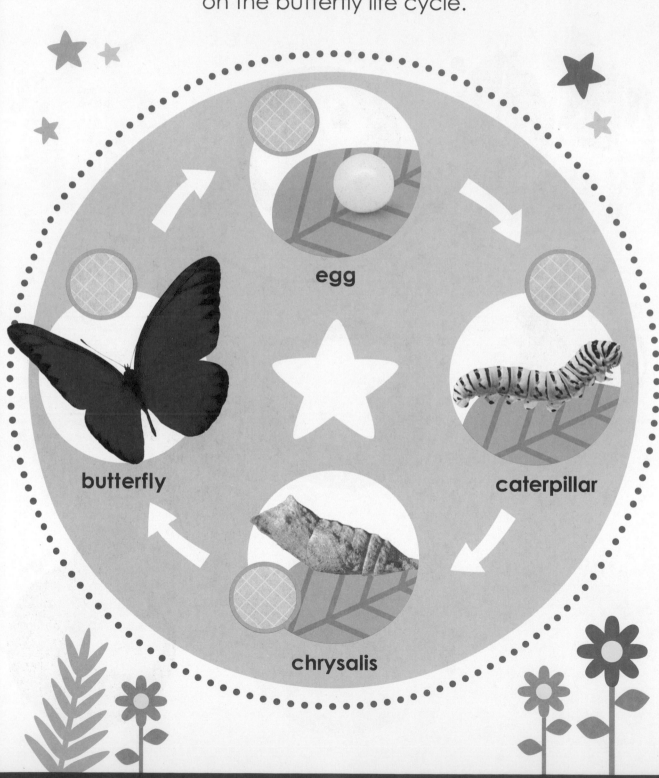

egg

butterfly

caterpillar

chrysalis

Frog life cycle

What comes first? Sticker the numbers **1** to **4**
on the frog life cycle.

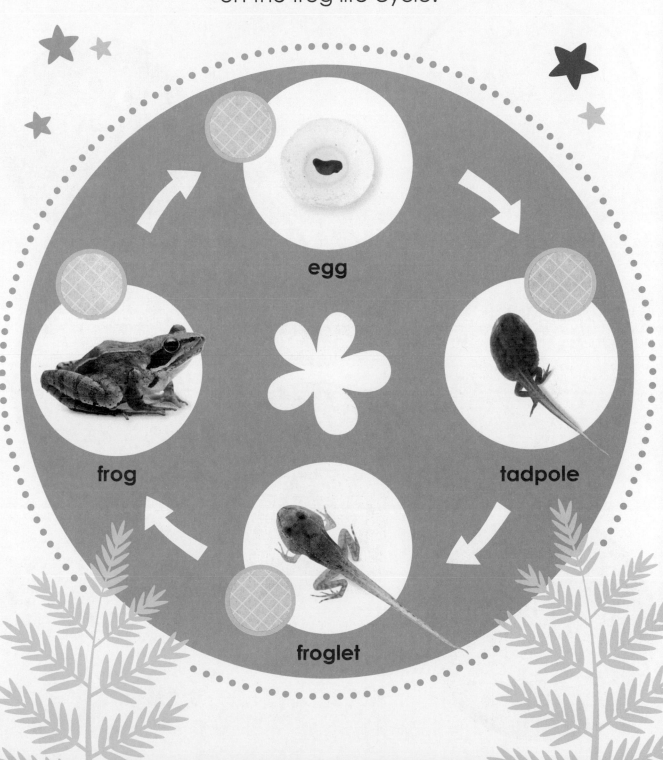

egg

tadpole

froglet

frog

Is it a plant?

Most plants have leaves. Circle all the plants.

Parts of a plant

Draw lines to show where each plant part is on the plant.

flower

fruit

leaf

stem

roots

Plants we eat

Eating food from plants keeps us healthy.
Color these foods the same colors as the dots.

Where does food come from?

Draw lines to join the food with where it comes from.

Hard or soft?

Circle the hard things with a **red** pencil.
Circle the soft things with a **blue** pencil.

Rough or smooth?

Circle the rough things with an **orange** pencil.
Circle the smooth things with a **green** pencil.

What's it made of?

Circle the things made of wood with a **purple** pencil.
Circle the things made of plastic with a yellow pencil.

What's it made of?

Circle the things made of metal with a **blue** pencil.
Circle the things made of glass with a **pink** pencil.

Tools that help us

Tools help us do things more easily.
Draw lines to join the tools with the activities.

shovel

cutting

ladder

climbing

scissors

digging

hammer

carrying

wheelbarrow

pushing

Sink or float

Color and sticker the boat **floating** on the water.

Color the treasure chest that has **sunk** to the bottom.

Day and night

Draw lines from the daytime things to the sun.
Draw lines from the nighttime things to the moon.

Hot and cold

Draw lines from the hot things to the fire.
Draw lines from the cold things to the snowflake.

Congratulations!

GOOD WORK AWARD!

Name: ....

has successfully completed the

Pre-K

Jumbo Workbook

Date: ....

Search this page for the stickers you need.

TRACING

Pages **4–5**

Pages **6–7**

Pages **8–9**

Pages **10–11**

Pages **12–13**

Pages **14–15**

Pages **16–17**

Pages **18–19**

Pages **22–23**

Pages **20–21**

Extra stickers

Search this page for the stickers you need.

MAZES

Pages **24–25**

Pages **26–27**

Pages **28–29**

Pages **30–31**

Pages **32–33**

Pages **34–35**

Pages **36–37**

Pages **38–39**

Pages **40–41**

Pages **42–43**

Extra stickers

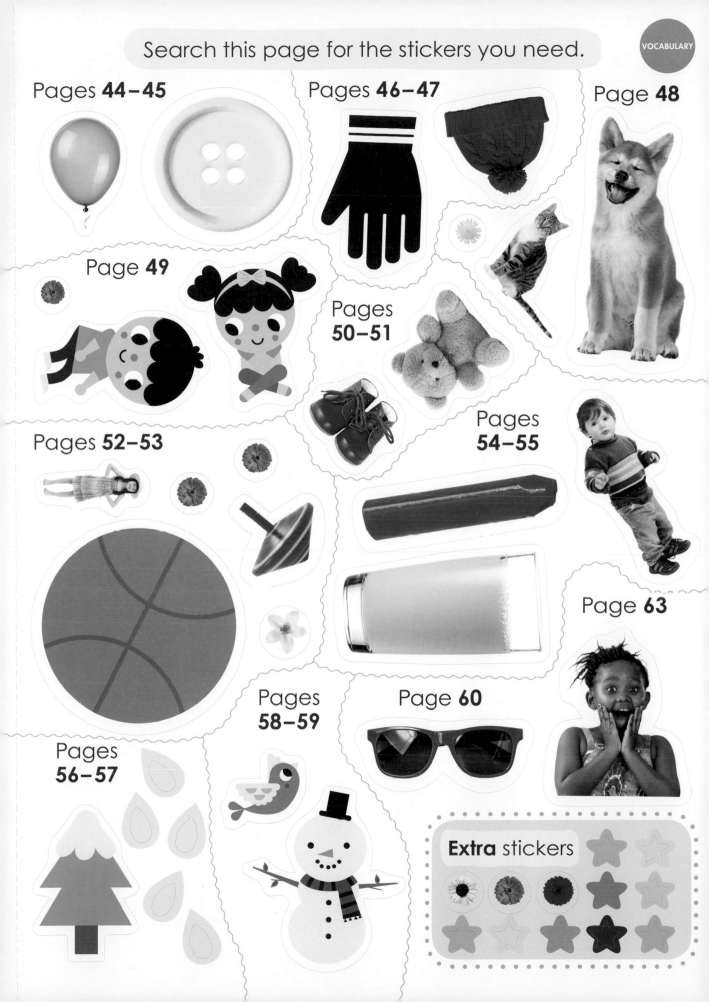

Search this page for the stickers you need.

VOCABULARY

Pages 44–45

Pages 46–47

Page 48

Page 49

Pages 50–51

Pages 52–53

Pages 54–55

Page 63

Pages 56–57

Pages 58–59

Page 60

Extra stickers

Search this page for the stickers you need.

LETTERS AND WORDS

Pages **64–65**

Pages **66–67**

Pages **72–73**

Pages **70–71**

Page **68**

Pages **76–77**

Pages **74–75**

Pages **80–81**

Pages **78–79**

Extra stickers

Search this page for the stickers you need.

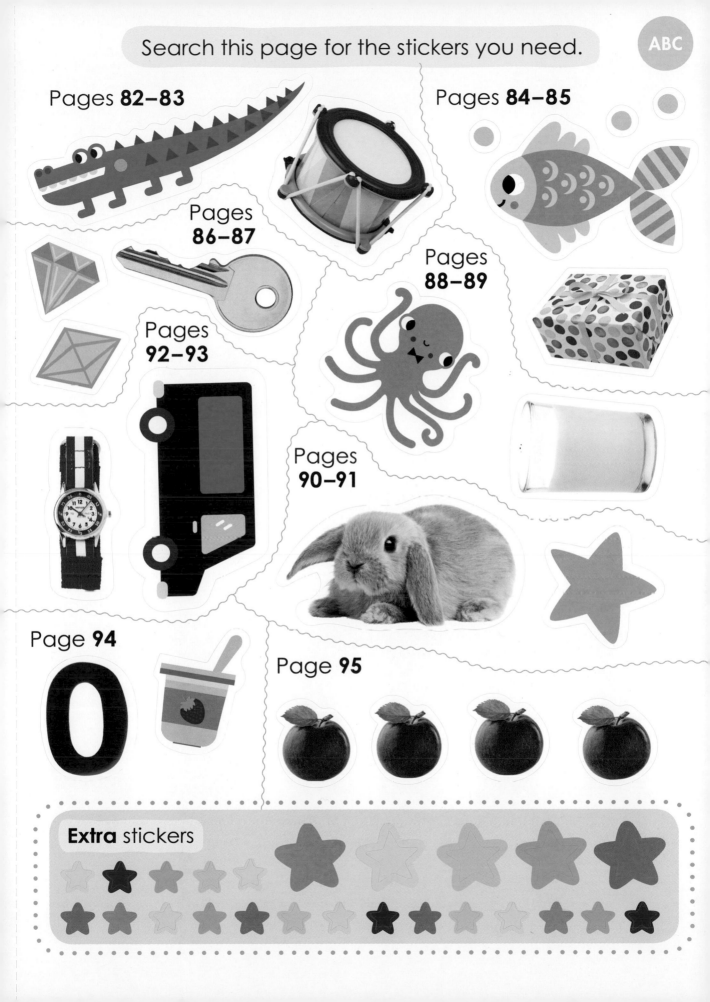

ABC

Pages **82–83**

Pages **84–85**

Pages **86–87**

Pages **88–89**

Pages **92–93**

Pages **90–91**

Page **94**

Page **95**

Extra stickers

Search this page for the stickers you need.

Pages 100–101

Pages 104–105

Pages 102–103

Pages 106–107

Pages 108–109

Pages 110–111

Pages 112–113

Pages 114–115

Pages 116–117

Pages 120–121

Extra stickers

Pages 118–119

Search this page for the stickers you need.

RHYMES

Pages **122–123**

Pages **124–125**

Pages **126–127**

Pages **128–129**

Pages **130–131**

Pages **132–133**

Pages **134–135**

Pages **136–137**

Pages **140–141**

Pages **138–139**

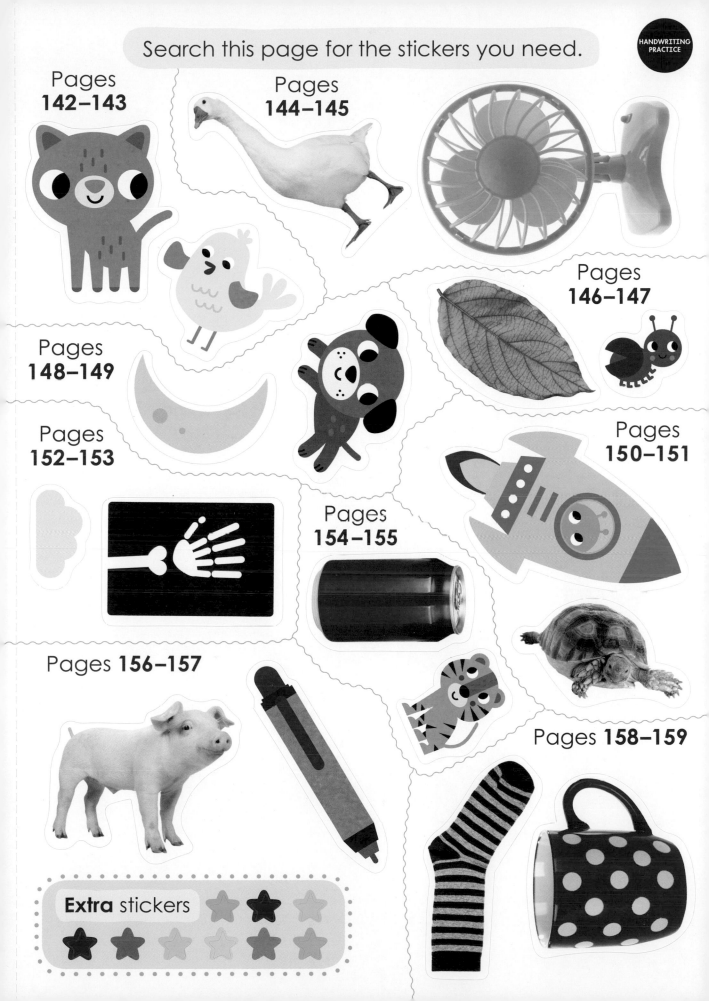

Search this page for the stickers you need.

Handwriting Practice

Pages 142–143

Pages 144–145

Pages 146–147

Pages 148–149

Pages 150–151

Pages 152–153

Pages 154–155

Pages 156–157

Pages 158–159

Extra stickers

Search this page for the stickers you need.

123

Pages **160–161**

Pages **162–163**

Pages **164–165**

Pages **166–167**

Pages **168–169**

Pages **170–171**

Pages **172–173**

Pages **174–175**

Pages **178–179**

Pages **176–177**

_R.O.B.O.T

Search this page for the stickers you need.

Page **180**

Page **182**

Page **184**

Page **186**

Page **188**

Pages **192–193**

Page **190**

Pages **194–195**

Pages **196–197**

Extra stickers

Search this page for the stickers you need.

SORTING

Pages 198–199

Pages 200–201

Pages 202–203

Pages 208–209

Page 205

Pages 210–211

Page 207

Page 214

Extra stickers

Page 217

Search this page for the stickers you need.

FIRST SCIENCE

Pages **218–219**

Pages **220–221**

4 2 3
1

Pages **222–223**

Pages **224–225**

Pages **226–227**

1 2 3
4 1 2
3
4

Pages **228–229**

Page **231**

Pages **238–239**

Page **237**

Certificate stickers